UNICORNS

DO YOU BELIEVE?

This series features creatures that excite our minds. They're magical. They're mythical. They're mysterious. They're also not real. They live in our stories. They're brought to life by our imaginations. Facts about these creatures are based on folklore, legends, and beliefs. We have a rich history of believing in the impossible. But these creatures only live in fantasies and dreams. Monsters do not live under our beds. They live in our heads!

45th Parallel Press

Published in the United States of America by Cherry Lake Publishing
Ann Arbor, Michigan
www.cherrylakepublishing.com

Reading Adviser: Marla Conn MS, Ed., Literacy specialist, Read-Ability, Inc.
Book Design: Felicia Macheske

Photo Credits: © Sari ONeal/Shutterstock.com, cover; © Marben/Shutterstock.com, 1; © Catmando/
Shutterstock.com, 5, 29; © Jannarong Kaewsuwan/Shutterstock.com, 8; © Fer Gregory/Shutterstock.com, 11;
© Nataliia Zhurbina/Shutterstock.com, 12; © CoreyFord/iStock, 15; © Kiselev Andrey Valerevich/
Shutterstock.com, 17; © Boris Ryaposov/Shutterstock.com, 18; © MFlynn/Shutterstock.com, 20; © Elenarts/
Shutterstock.com, 23; © Elle Arden Images/Shutterstock.com, 24; © Renata Sedmakova/Shutterstock.com, 27

Graphic Elements Throughout: © denniro/Shutterstock.com; © Libellule/Shutterstock.com; © sociologas/
Shutterstock.com; © paprika/Shutterstock.com; © ilolab/Shutterstock.com; © Bruce Rolff/Shutterstock.com

45th Parallel Press is an imprint of Cherry Lake Publishing.

Library of Congress Cataloging-in-Publication Data

Names: Loh-Hagan, Virginia, author.
Title: Unicorns : magic, myth, and mystery / by Virginia Loh-Hagan.
Description: Ann Arbor : Cherry Lake Publishing, [2016] | Series: Magic,
 myth, and mystery | Includes bibliographical references and index.
Identifiers: LCCN 2016004925| ISBN 9781634711159 (hardcover) | ISBN
 9781634713139 (pbk.) | ISBN 9781634712149 (pdf) | ISBN 9781634714129
 (ebook)
Subjects: LCSH: Unicorns—Juvenile literature. | Animals, Mythical—Juvenile
 literature.
Classification: LCC GR830.U6 L64 2016 | DDC 398.24/54—dc23
LC record available at http://lccn.loc.gov/2016004925

Cherry Lake Publishing would like to acknowledge the work of The Partnership for 21st Century Skills.
Please visit www.p21.org for more information.

Printed in the United States of America
Corporate Graphics Inc.

TABLE of CONTENTS

One Special Horn

**What are unicorns? What do they look like?
What are different types of unicorns?**

"Do you believe in magic?" Unicorns are magical.
They look like horses. But they're taller. They're
white. They have blue **hooves**. Hooves are tough
coverings. They cover the feet of some animals.

Unicorns have a single horn. It's called an
alicorn. It's straight. It's shaped like a spiral. It
comes out of their foreheads. It can be white, gold,
black, or rainbow. It has a gemstone at the base.
It's their power source.

Unicorns sometimes have blue eyes. They can have silver manes and tails. They shine brightly in the sun. Some have a goat beard. Some have lion tails.

The spiral keeps the alicorn straight.

When Fantasy Meets Reality!

A Danish throne was made of "unicorn horns." Queen Elizabeth I had a "unicorn horn." But they were fakes. The horns were actually narwhal **tusks**. Tusks are teeth that are like horns. Narwhals are whales. They live in Arctic waters. Male narwhals have one extended tusk. (Some females have it. But their tusks are smaller. They're less spiraled.) The tusk shoots out from the mouth. It's spiraled. It's made of ivory. It keeps growing. It's between 5 and 10 feet (1.5 and 3 meters) long. It's hollow. It weighs about 22 pounds (10 kilograms). It has a lot of nerves. It's sensitive. One in 500 males has two tusks. Narwhals are the unicorns of the sea.

Pegasus didn't have an alicorn.

Some unicorns fly. They have wings. They're different from Pegasus. Pegasus was a winged **stallion**. A stallion is an adult male horse. Pegasus was godly. Poseidon was his father. Poseidon was the king of seas and horses. His mother was Medusa. Medusa was an evil witch. She had snakes for hair. Pegasus is white. He'd hit the land with his hoof. He created water springs this way.

Unicorns aren't in Greek stories. But people report **sightings**. They've done this throughout history. Sightings are when people see things. Unicorns are in stories, art, and songs.

Chinese unicorns have deer bodies. They have an ox tail. They have horse hooves. They have dragon heads. They have green fish scales. They fly. They have curved alicorns. Their alicorns pierce guilty people's hearts.

Persian unicorns are warriors. They have rhino bodies. They have lion tails. They have six eyes. They have nine mouths. They change shape. They have curved golden alicorns.

Indian unicorns look like donkeys. They have red heads. They have white bodies. They have blue eyes. Their alicorns are 18 inches (46 centimeters) long.

There are Eastern unicorns and Western unicorns.

Chapter Two

Magical and Pure

Why are unicorn horns special? How are other unicorn body parts special? What are the powers of unicorns?

Unicorns are pure. This makes their power strong. Their alicorns are super powerful. They cure sickness. They **purify** poisoned water. Purify means to make clean. Alicorns protect against evil. They ensure long and healthy lives.

Alicorns are harder than diamonds. They're weapons. They're like **lances**. Lances are sharp poles. Alicorns gore enemies. They spear them. They **impale** them. Impale means to ram with a pole. Unicorns fight to defend themselves. They don't attack. They don't hunt. They don't need to eat. They soak in the power of the sun.

Alicorns were made into cups. This took away any poisons.

Unicorn blood is thick. It's silver. People want to drink it. It stops people from dying. But there's a cost. Drinking unicorn blood causes a **cursed** life. Curses mean bad things happen. Killing unicorns is evil. Blood that touches the ground is deadly. It kills anything that touches it.

Unicorn tears heal wounds. They heal broken hearts. Unicorn livers cure sicknesses. Wearing unicorn skin keeps bodies healthy.

Unicorns are beautiful. But their looks kill. It's dangerous to look at them. Their pureness hurts eyes. Unicorns control minds. They make people do things for them.

Almost all parts of the unicorn are powerful.

Explained by Science!

Unicorn horn magic can be explained by bezoar stones. Bezoar stones are hairballs. Sometimes, animals swallow bits that can't be digested. Digest means to break down. The bits don't pass through bodies. They stay in the stomach. They catch other bits. They form blobs. They become stones. They're known as bezoars. Bezoars were believed to fight poison. People put bezoar stones in their drinks. (Bezoar means "antidote," or a cure.) Bezoar stones have brushite. Brushite reacts against arsenic. Arsenic is a poison. Bezoar stones are common in young children and horses.

Even dreaming about unicorns gives people power.

Unicorns are sensitive. They feel shadows. They tread lightly. They **hover**. They don't touch the ground. They don't leave hoofprints. They don't harm anything on the ground.

They have sweet voices. They sound like wind chimes. They read minds. They speak to all creatures. They tame everything around them. They control rain. They control fire.

They're **immortal**. They live forever. Only evil can kill them. Unicorns always reach their destinations, even when hunted. They don't fall into pits or traps. They're lucky. They're smart.

Chapter Three

Hunted

Why are unicorns hunted?
What are the weaknesses of unicorns?

Unicorns once roamed freely. Then humans discovered their magic. A person who sees a unicorn is granted a wish. A person who touches a unicorn will be happy forever.

Some humans became unicorn hunters. They wanted the unicorns' magic. Unicorns die when their alicorns are removed. They lose who they are. They're touched by evil.

So, unicorns went into hiding. They're impossible

to find. They're impossible to catch. They'd rather die than be captured. They won't come back until evil is gone.

Unicorns are difficult animals to hunt. They have many powers.

Unicorn hunters use maidens as bait.

Unicorns have weaknesses. They're not fighters. They don't hurt others.

They like **maidens**. Maidens are pure women. They go to maidens. They rest their heads in maidens' laps.

Unicorns are good at hiding. But they're easy to see. Their coats catch the sun. They reflect rays. This gives them an **aura**. An aura is a light. It's around their bodies. Some alicorns change colors. The colors reflect the unicorns' moods.

SURVIVAL TIPS!

- Trick unicorns into running into a tree. Their horns will get stuck.

- Bring a fair maiden. Unicorns will get distracted.

- Don't run toward unicorns. They'll lower their heads. They'll gore you.

- Stay away from their hooves. They'll attack.

- Bring a lot of people. Unicorns will hide. They won't come out.

- Don't look at unicorns in the eyes. Don't be a threat. Let them come to you.

- Don't turn your back to unicorns. Walk calmly ahead. Don't run. This draws attention.

- Ask permission to approach unicorns. Unicorns must give consent. They can't be tamed.

Unicorns live alone. Or they live in small groups. They don't go to open spaces. They live in magical forests. The forest protects them. They live near clear lakes. They need to see themselves. They're vain. They're the most beautiful creatures in the world. And they know it.

Some unicorns want to be shinier. They kill sun dogs. These creatures have shiny coats. These unicorns aren't pure. They lose their powers.

Lions and unicorns are enemies.

Chapter Four

Becoming Pure

What are some ideas about where unicorns came from?

Some believe unicorns are the first animals to be created. Unicorns sprung from the earth's center. They're perfect. They're pure. They're gentle. They're free. They're peaceful. They're born from goodness.

Some believe unicorns are related to Elasmotherium. This was a huge rhino. It lived around Asia. It had an alicorn. It lived during the Ice Age.

No one really knows how unicorns came to be.

Some people worship a sun god. These people believe unicorns are God's animals. According to them, unicorn females find **mates**. Mates are partners. They go find a baby unicorn together.

A high goddess dreams a unicorn. She does this when a unicorn is needed. The unicorn couple gets one of these newly dreamt unicorns. They take care of the baby unicorn. They teach the baby unicorn. They protect the baby unicorn.

Unicorns are too special to be born like other animals.

Know the Lingo!

- **Barrel:** area of a unicorn's body between the front legs and the back legs

- **Buck:** leaping into the air with the head lowered and the back arched

- **Carbuncle:** the gemstone at the base of a unicorn's horn

- **Coruu:** a horn

- **Dock:** bony part of a unicorn's tail from which hair grows

- **Einhorn:** German unicorn

- **Karkadann:** Persian unicorn

- **Nearside:** left-hand side of the unicorn

- **Offside:** right-hand side of the unicorn

- **Poll:** highest point on the top of a unicorn's head

- **Qilin:** Chinese unicorn

- **Re'em:** "wild ox," another word for unicorn

- **Unus:** one

Chapter Five

Believing in Magic

What is an example of a unicorn sighting?
What is a popular story about unicorns?

Ctesias was an ancient Greek doctor. He traveled. He wrote about special creatures. These creatures looked like horses. They had white bodies. They had red heads. They had blue eyes. They had alicorns. More unicorn sightings followed his stories.

Many unicorn stories feature maidens. There's a princess. She's the most beautiful person. She walks in the forest. It gets dark. She gets lost. She sees a unicorn. The unicorn knows she's pure. They go to the castle. Soldiers try to capture the unicorn. The princess saves the unicorn. The unicorn runs away. It's never seen again.

Unicorn stories are often very similar.

Real-World Connection

Liang Xiuzhen lives in China. She's elderly. Some call her the "Unicorn Woman." She has a strange growth on her head. The growth looks like a large horn. The horn started as a black mole. It was itchy. It grew into a small horn. Xiuzhen broke it off. But the horn quickly grew back. It's over 5 inches (12.7 cm) long. Xiuzhen's son said, "Now the horn hurts my mother and prevents her from sleeping." Doctors said Xiuzhen has cornu cutaneum. This is a skin tumor.

Unicorns are allowed to go to Eden once every century. Eden renews the unicorn's strength.

Some people faked alicorns. People created tests to check for real alicorns. They threw the horns in water. True alicorns bubble and boil. They put poisonous plants nearby. True alicorns sweat. They poisoned a bird. True alicorns save the bird. They drew a circle with the horn. They put a spider inside the circle. True alicorns wouldn't let spiders cross the circle. They put the horn in a pot with four scorpions. True alicorns would kill the scorpions.

True or false? Doesn't matter. Unicorns mystify.

Did You Know?

- In some stories, unicorns are goats.

- Alexander the Great said he rode a unicorn.

- King Francis I of France wanted a unicorn horn. He wanted protection against his wife. His wife was Catherine de Medici. Some thought Catherine was a witch. She used poisons.

- Asian cultures believe in four sacred creatures. These creatures are unicorns, dragons, phoenixes, and tortoises.

- There was a great flood. Noah built an ark. He took two of every kind of animal. He forgot to take the unicorns. Some believe that's why they don't exist anymore.

- Genghis Khan attacked India. Then, he met a unicorn. The unicorn bowed to him. He thought it was a sign from his dead father. He stopped attacking India.

- According to the Harry Potter stories, powerful wands are made with unicorn hair.

- Unicorn horns were made into powder. The powder was sold in stores. Whole unicorn horns were kept in vaults. Vaults are safes.

- The Unicorn Cave is in Germany's Harz Mountains. People found bones there. They thought they were unicorn bones.

- Female unicorns grow shorter horns.

- Lake Superior State University is in Michigan. It gives permits to hunt unicorns.

Consider This!

Take a Position: Unicorn hunters were real. They believed unicorns existed. They looked for unicorns. Do you think unicorns should have been hunted? Argue your point with reasons and evidence.

Say What? Unicorns are magical. They can't be captured. But they have fewer defenses than regular monsters. Explain how unicorns can fight against unicorn hunters.

Think About It! Some say unicorns aren't monsters. Some say they are. What do you think? How would you define a monster? Do unicorns fit your definition of monsters? Explain your thinking.

Learn More

- Alexander, Skye. *Unicorns: The Myths, Legends, and Lore*. Avon, MA: Adams Media, 2015.

- All About Unicorns: www.allaboutunicorns.com

- Hamilton, John. *Unicorns and Other Magical Creatures*. Edina, MN: ABDO Publications, 2005.

- Sautter, A. J. *A Field Guide to Griffins, Unicorns, and Other Mythical Beasts*. Mankato, MN: Capstone Press, 2015.

Glossary

alicorn (AH-lih-korn) single, spiraled horn coming out of a unicorn's forehead

aura (OR-uh) a light around a body

cursed (KURSD) having bad things happen

hooves (HOOVZ) tough covering around animals' feet, like toenails

hover (HUHV-ur) to be slightly above the ground

immortal (ih-MOR-tuhl) able to live forever

impale (im-PAYL) to pierce through with a sharp pole

lances (LANS-iz) long, sharp poles

maidens (MAY-duhnz) pure women

mates (MAYTS) partners

purify (PYOOR-uh-fye) to make clean by removing poisons

sightings (SITE-ingz) reports of seeing unicorns

stallion (STAL-yuhn) male horse that can still breed

tusks (TUHSKS) long, curved, pointed teeth that are like horns

Index

About the Author

Dr. Virginia Loh-Hagan is an author, university professor, former classroom teacher, and curriculum designer. One of her favorite childhood movies was *The Last Unicorn*. She lives in San Diego with her very tall husband and very naughty dogs. To learn more about her, visit www.virginialoh.com.